J. M. STUDEBAKER

TO OLD HANGTOWN
OR BUST

PILGRIMAGE
OF
J. M. STUDEBAKER
TO
THE PLACE WHERE HE MADE HIS FIRST STAKE
AND GOT HIS START IN LIFE

REPORTED BY
WELLS DRURY

Printed for Private Circulation
by the Reception Committee
Placerville, California
1912

Notice

In many older books, foxing (or discoloration) occurs and, in some instances, print lightens with wear and age. Reprinted books, such as this, often duplicate these flaws, notwithstanding efforts to reduce or eliminate them. The pages of this reprint have been digitally enhanced and, where possible, the flaws eliminated in order to provide clarity of content and a pleasant reading experience.

To Old Hangtown or Bust
[El Dorado County, California]

Originally published
Placerville, California
1912

Copyright © 2010 Janaway Publishing, Inc.

Reprinted With New Index.
by:

Janaway Publishing, Inc.
732 Kelsey Ct.
Santa Maria, California 93454
(805) 925-1038
www.janawaygenealogy.com

2010

ISBN 10: 1-59641-195-3
ISBN 13: 978-1-59641-195-1

Made in the United States of America

CROSSING THE PLAINS

"I stand upon the green Sierra's wall;
Against the east, beyond the yellow grass,
I see the hill-tops rise and fall,——
          *   *   *   *   *
There lies the Nation's great white way of death.

My brave and unremebered heroes, rest;
You fell in silence, silent lie in sleep.

The desert winds, they whistle by and sweep
About you; browned and russet grasses wave
Along a thousand leagues that lie one common grave.

The proud and careless pass in palace car
Along the road you blazoned white with bones;
Pass swift to people, and possess, and mar
Your lands with monuments and lettered stones
Unto themselves. Thank God! this waste disowns
Their touch. His everlasting hand has drawn
A shining line around you. Wealth bemoans
The waste your splendid grave employs. Sleep on,
No hand shall touch your dust this side of God and Dawn."

                                    —*Joaquin Miller.*

GROUP OF HANGTOWN PIONEERS

FROM A PHOTOGRAPH TAKEN AT PLACERVILLE, CALIFORNIA, APRIL 16, 1912

OLD HANGTOWN was in happy mood, Tuesday, the 16th of April, 1912, in honor of the return of J. M. Studebaker, President of the Studebaker Corporation of South Bend, Indiana, who had traveled across the continent to pay a farewell visit to the place where he got his start in life, and laid the foundation for the competency which he now enjoys. This home-coming was the fulfillment of a promise made by Studebaker to himself and his friends half a century ago.

The streets were in holiday attire. Garlands hung above the sidewalks, made of fragrant boughs from the pine trees of the hillsides, enriched with golden California poppies.

```
┌─────────────────────────────────────────┐
│     WE ARE GLAD YOU CAME BACK             │
└─────────────────────────────────────────┘
```

Said the printed placards that were to be seen in the windows of stores and homes. From the ravines of the premier mining county of the Golden State, which bears and deserves the name "El Dorado" because gold was here discovered, and still streams from its hills and bars and canyons, came the surviving pioneers of the district. In joyful expectancy they hastened to Placerville (which in its pristine glory was known to fame as Old Hangtown), all glad to greet the friend of their young manhood. They were proud to renew the fraternal bonds which joined them together so closely in the opening days of this great commonwealth.

PIONEER'S PIOUS PILGRIMAGE.

Studebaker began the final stages of his pilgrimage from San Francisco, where he got in touch with a handful of former Hangtowners. Stephen T. Gage, of Oakland; Daniel W. Earl, of San Francisco; Alexander P. Murgotten, of San Jose; William Bell, of Oakland, and Charles H. Townsend, of Berkeley, with Studebaker, completed the party.

The trip up the Sacramento river by the steamer Seminole gave time for these pioneers to exchange stories concerning their experiences, and they did not spare one another in recalling incidents grotesque or tragic, which punctuated the early history of the State, and in which one or more of their number bore part. Everybody had a nickname in those halcyon days, and Studebaker's was "Wheelbarrow John," because of his fame in producing a miners' wheelbarrow after his own design, which proved superior to all others in that district.

Nothing that happened less than fifty years ago was permitted as a topic of conversation.

All had been members of the old Confidence Engine
Company of Hangtown, and they all remembered when
the Orleans Hotel was burned. McKean Buchanan was
playing "Richelieu" that night, and he rushed from the
stage with his cardinal's robes flowing in the wind and
seizing the pump-bar of the old hand-engine helped the
firemen to throw water on the blazing building. Everybody agreed on that occurrence, but singularly when it
came to personal experiences there were divergencies
in their recollections. The several versions were some-
times far apart. But who could be expected to remember
some trifling incident more than five decades old, es-
pecially if he happened to get the worst of a practical
joke, or something of that kind?

GENUINE COMRADESHIP.

They call one another by their first names, John, Steve,
Dan, Bill, Aleck and Charley, with the easy familiarity
of boys let loose from school. It is genuine, this com-
radeship, because the absolute equality of pioneer days and
customs never can be obliterated. As for this trip, it
is Studebaker's treat, and that is all. Nobody refers to
it, and nobody thinks of it as particularly odd or re-
markable in any degree. It is just as if in the early
days one of the gold diggers had made a lucky strike
in the placers, and coming to town for a celebration
had "set 'em up for the boys." This keeping up of old
memories and the old-fashioned sentiment of friendship
is refreshing. It is eloquent of that charming frankness
with which each individual dealt with his fellow beings
in that era of virile virtues of the Pioneer, when everything was on the level — open and aboveboard — when
everybody knew everybody else, and a man was judged
by his character and not by his coat.

Studebaker shows acquaintance with current happenings in California from the time of his first arrival at
Hangtown to the present. He knows about the mines,
has followed the industrial and manufacturing conditions,
and is familiar with the writings of Bret Harte, Joaquin

Miller, Mark Twain, and the authors of the original Overland Monthly school. He has retained his youthful enthusiasm, and interest in the welfare of those about him, and is as fine a specimen of whole-souled, genial, unspoiled humanity as you would wish to meet on a pleasant day's journey.

BOXED WITH YANKEE SULLIVAN.

"Let's see, Wheelbarrow John, weren't you the lad who tried to knock out Yankee Sullivan, the famous prize-fighter, when he was living in Hangtown?" quizzed Earl.

"Not exactly," answered Studebaker.

"Maybe I'm mistaken, but I thought you were that individual. Seems to me some of the boys thought you were big and strong enough, and had the sand to pose as the hope of the white race about that time," Earl persisted.

"Now see here, Dan, what's the use of talking about that. But if you must keep it up, we might as well get it straight. It was just this way, and you know it. Together with yourself and a lot of other Hangtown boys we began to take boxing lessons from Yankee Sullivan at a dollar a lesson, and the first time I put on the gloves he told me to hit him right on the nose as hard as I could. I thought he meant it, so I let out my fist with all my strength. What happened was that my fist never touched his nose, but, Yankee Sullivan style, his fist touched mine, which made me turn a double somersault and see stars in the daytime. I never took another lesson. Sullivan was a tough, and when he got to San Francisco he imagined the Vigilantes were after him, and he cut the main artery in his arm and bled to death. You old-timers must remember that."

Dan agreed that John was about right.

BOOTS ATTRACT GOLD BRICKS.

"Well, if Steve isn't wearing boots," exclaimed Studebaker, as Gage put his feet on the radiator in the smoking room.

"Boots! Of course I'm wearing boots. What do you suppose a gentleman would wear?"

"Oh, that's all right, to be sure; but just the same, that's the first pair of boots I've seen on a man's feet since I left California."

"Never wore anything else, and never will," Gage shot back.

"No objection on my part, no objection at all; but when you get to any of the big cities back east, I want to advise you that you'd better look out or the gang will try to sell you a gold brick," said Studebaker laughingly. "On my soul, I believe that if you should land even in South Bend wearing those boots there would be bunco-steerers travel hundreds of miles to offer you some get-rich-quick proposition."

"So they did," assented Gage, "but they soon let go when I told them that if they would wait until I could get at my satchel, I'd show them that I had a few bricks of my own."

BLUSHED AT TOO MUCH PRAISE.

"Billy Bell was reputed to be the most mischevious boy in Hangtown," said Murgotten gravely, and the white haired man thus pointed out actually blushed with delight at the compliment. "He was known at that time as the drummer boy, and has continued his habit of being an entertainer by supplying the rising generation of San Francisco with more bird-whistles than any other person on the coast," resumed Murgotten. "Billy was a clever scrapper, a regular tough nut, and so brave that he never saw a fellow big enough to scare him. He used to lead us to the upper town to fight the gang up there, and though he usually came out all right with his particular engagement, the rest of us nearly always got beautifully licked."

Bell smiled approval of this historical narration, and apropos of nothing in particular, musingly remarked that the fare from San Francisco to Sacramento on the steamer used to be an ounce of gold (worth about $16)

except when there was opposition, and then it would
go down to 25 cents.

The Lee & Marshall circus was the topic which
brought up a vast number of recollections. Townsend
recalled that several men who afterwards became prominent in public affairs made their first appearance with
that prodigious aggregation of world-wonders.

THROWING THE DIAMOND HITCH.

"You were rather fond of circuses in those days,
Steve," Townsend ventured, addressing Gage.

"Yes, and I like 'em yet," was the answer.

"I remember seeing you throwing the diamond hitch
over a buckskin pack-mule," added Townsend.

"That's no lie," said Gage, "and I can throw the diamond yet. I had as fine a train of pack-mules as ever
crossed the grade. At least that's my impression. I
never say a thing is so any more. All I venture to do
is to give my impression. I bought those mules at Marys-
ville for $5000 cash. That was in the winter of '59 and
'60, when the Comstock lode was drawing thousands of
people that way. It was hard work but it paid. In 83
days I cleared $10,400 in twenty-dollar pieces, packing
freight to Virginia City.

"The great Comstock lode was discovered in the sum-
mer of 1859, and immediately attracted a great many people from California. They wintered in Virginia City, and
early in the season all the stores ran short of provisions,
including whisky, so freight prices went ballooning. Pack-
ers got whatever they felt like charging for all the goods
they could get over the snow-blocked trails. I frequently
met Snowshoe Thompson, the famous mail carrier, on the
road between Hangtown and the Comstock."

LEGEND OF STRAWBERRY VALLEY.

The legend of how Strawberry Valley got its name
came up for discussion as usual. Hank Monk, during his
lifetime, always insisted that the name was derived from
the keeper of a way station. "That son of a buzzard,"
drawled Hank, "used to steal the oats and barley from

the horses of the teamsters, and put straw in place of the grain, so we all called him 'Straw' Berry, which stuck to the station; and that's how Strawberry Valley got its name."

"No such thing," Gage declared. "I was there long before Hank Monk, and saw the strawberries growing on the spot where the station was afterwards built. The house was right in the midst of the strawberry patch, and that was why it was called Strawberry Valley."

MINERS' LAWS SUPREME.

Like everybody in those days, these six pioneers worked placer claims. Studebaker said his first claim was 25x25 feet in size, and he did fairly well. He said that he still has in his possession $700 worth of the coarse gold taken by him out of the American river, near Hangtown.

Gage's claim was 16x16 feet in size, and proved profitable.

"Not all my mining ventures were satisfactory," said Gage. "There were months when I didn't make expenses. The best I did was to take out $50 a day for six weeks. The local regulations made by the miners were the supreme law of the land, and from them there was no appeal. Apparently such a thing was never thought of by anybody. Tenure of claims depended on actual occupation and use. The specific rules differed in the different districts. If a miner left his claim for the time provided for in the rules of his district he lost all right and title to it. He could sell his right, but if a claim was left without any person in possession it could be taken up by the next man who in good faith went to work on it, as actual use of the land was absolutely necessary. It could not be held idle. But woe betide the man who tried to jump a claim legally held by another. Claim-jumpers were decidedly unpopular, and according to my impression they were few and far between. The best laws for gold mining in the world grew out of the miners' rules in California, just as the laws governing silver

mining were developed from the regulations of the Nevada miners in regard to the working of the ledges in
that State."

SURPASSES THE VALLEY OF THE NILE.

"The last time I traversed this river before my departure for my home in Indiana in 1858," said Studebaker, "it
was a wilderness. No traces of human habitation that
I can remember. Now it is one of the most productive
valleys that I ever saw. It surpasses the valley of the
Nile. As far as the eye can reach we see vineyards, and
orchards and asparagus fields, and everything that the
heart can wish. I thought I had kept in touch with the
advancement of California, but this development even
in this one valley passes my expectations. It is impres-
sive, marvelous. Captain B. N. Rideout of the steamer
Seminole has shown me a map of the rest of the Sacramento valley, with a stream of water navigable 200 miles
above Sacramento, and with the great San Joaquin river
stretching to the south. No wonder your State is growing so rapidly. But it seems to me that it has just begun
to grow. Very few people see these splendid valleys, because they come and go by railroad and they have no
realization of your natural resources. If these resources
ever become generally known there will be such a rush
for California that those already here will be but a
handful compared to the population which you will have
within a few years.

"Sacramento always was a prosperous city and always
will be. Its location is so favorable that nothing ever
can interfere with its progress. I am not surprised to
learn that it has gone ahead marvelously in the last few
years. Its stability cannot be disputed and all oldtimers
rejoice in its development. The annals of Sacramento
occupy a large place in the history of California, and
that is one reason why the oldtimers look upon it with
so much affection.

"Then there's San Francisco that was a straggling
town of sand dunes when I sailed away through the Golden

Gate so many years ago, but which now rivals the fore-
most cities of the world. Of course I have visited California since my departure, but I can scarcely realize that
the present city has been rebuilt in six years. It is all
wonderful, and you Californians have a right to feel proud
of what you have done, and to rejoice in what you are
bound to do in the years to come."

Studebaker gave much consideration to Alameda county,
looking with admiration on the progress of Oakland, with
its new harbor improvements. The location of Berkeley,
its wide area of level land for factories and warehouses
attracted his favorable attention.

LESSON IN ADVERTISING.

"In those early days," Studebaker continued, "I never
saw Los Angeles, though I heard of it, and now everybody has heard of it. There is not a better known city
on earth than Los Angeles, and the way in which Los Angeles is forging ahead is an object lesson of judicious
advertising, and then having the goods to back up your
claims. It is just the same story, from every part of
California. The natural advantages are attracting more
people, and with this additional population the fullest development of the country will be fulfilled."

BRAVING DANGERS OF THE OCEAN.

"We had some excitement at the time I started home
by way of the isthmus. We sailed on the old steamer
Golden Gate, and when we were out three days she broke
her shaft and it took us six days to get back. The only
available vessel in the harbor was an old steamer that
had been declared unseaworthy, and it was thought dan-
gerous to go in her. The captain said he was willing to
take the risk if we were, but he would carry only 1500
passengers instead of 3200 that started in the Golden
Gate. Two of my comrades, the Coleman brothers, one
having $3000 and the other $8000, changed their plans after
their return to San Francisco. There was great excitement over rich gold discoveries reported to have been
made in the Frazer river country, so instead of going with
me to their home in Schenectady, New York State, they

joined in the rush for Frazer river, lost all their money, and died poor."

A TOUCH OF SENTIMENT.

At Sacramento Studebaker's attention was called to copies of the Sacramento Union and the Bee, and he spoke interestingly of the days when he knew Jim Anthony, Paul Morrill and James McClatchy, who were prominent in pioneer journalism.

Replying to a question he said: "So you would like to know what prompts me to make this trip to Old Hangtown, would you? Well, this may be the last time that I shall have a chance to see these old boys, and I just wanted to meet them around the table once more. We are getting along in years, some of us, and like to talk over what happened when we were younger. Sentiment? Yes, it must be sentiment, or something of that kind, that makes me do this. You may call this sentiment a grateful remembrance of the place where I made my stake with which to begin business for myself. So I want to go back to the old stamping ground for a day and a night, and indulge in a last look at the place where my early friendships were formed. I want to clasp hands with companions who knew me then, and who have been my friends through all these years. Our lives have led us far apart, but I have never forgotten them, and it is a pleasure to think that they have not forgotten me."

There was an incident at the Hotel Sacramento, unimportant in itself, but truly characteristic, which illustrated the fine feeling of respect for womankind which universally prevailed in the early period of the American settlement, and which survives among the Pioneers and their descendants. At the second floor an aged woman who was so infirm that she had to support herself with a cane, got in the elevator. Instantly every head was uncovered, and two of the party standing next the door reached out to offer assistance. It was the unconscious courtesy that springs from the spontaneous promptings of a chivalrous nature.

From Sacramento to Placerville the pilgrimage was continued by automobile, Studebaker's touring car marked with the Studebaker number, "010-71-Ind," being ready for the run. The splendid boulevard from Sacramento to Folsom, a distance of 22 miles, delighted the visitor, who as a maker of automobiles realized the advantages of such a perfect thoroughfare. Those joining the party at Sacramento were Chester N. Weaver, Thomas B. Richards, and J. M. S. Johnson, the latter a grandson of Studebaker.

THROUGH SYLVAN VISTAS.

The road from Folsom to Placerville passes through a country which so far as pertains to the forest is as primitive in appearance as if fresh from the creative forces. The road bed in spots is hard and smooth, reminiscent of the era when Charley McClane was division superintendent of the Pioneer Stage Line, and such wizard drivers as Hank Monk, Curly Bill Gearhardt, Newt Spencer, Billy Hodges, Big Jake, Baldy Green and others of that class, guided their teams of four or six wild bronchos along these grades. The hand of man has made but little impression on the trees that line the highway. They are the same as when they sheltered Murietta and Vasquez and other bandits, lying in wait to rob plethoric miners bearing gold dust from the diggings, or to pillage a Wells-Fargo treasure-box. This road once teemed with thousands of emigrants. Eating-houses, stables for teamsters and stage-stations were numerous. In the drive through this mountainous region the fleet-footed jack-rabbit and the crested quail were frequently seen darting across the road; noisy bluejays, and blackbirds with cardinal chevrons on their wings, and woodpeckers pecking on the old barn door were in evidence. But this primitive state is doomed to be speedily changed. Already this road is traversed daily by many automobiles and teams, and soon this traffic will be materially augmented, because this piece of road will be made a smooth highway, as it is to be part of the $18,000,000 Camino Real which is

planned by the State of California to connect all parts of
the commonwealth.

PICTURESQUE SCENES GLADDEN THE EYES.

The sun shone brightly and in the distance light
clouds hung in feathery whiteness above the snow-cov-
ered spurs of the Sierra Nevada mountains that dominate
the landscape. Meadow larks springing from the man-
zanitas along the roadway warbled their welcome. The
red madronos were ranged below the wild olive trees, and
it is here that the

—"Rabbits play, and the quail all day
Pipe on the chapparal hill."

A more perfect day never was enjoyed in any clime.
Not even the far-famed Riviera can rival California in
the early spring time.

FREEDOM OF THE CITY TENDERED TO VISITOR.

When the Middletown oaks were reached the visitors
were met by a delegation of Placerville citizens, headed
by Mayor J. C. O'Donnell, son of a Hangtown pioneer,
and the freedom of the city was tendered to Studebaker.

Up through the streets the automobiles dashed, and
from every side there were cheers for the only success-
ful pioneer who had ever made a point of returning to
Old Hangtown to show his appreciation of the camp
which afforded him a first firm foothold this side of the
plains and the mountains.

The verbal exchanges between the residents of the
town and the visitor were genuinely heart-felt.

"SAY, DO YOU REMEMBER?"

Reminiscences were in order when the grizzled men
joined hands at the rendezvous prepared by the committee.

"Here's Dan Earl who always was a crank about good
roads," exclaimed Charley Weatherwax, who supported
himself with a crutch and a cane, and insisted that he
was growing younger because formerly he had been com-
pelled to use two crutches. Then it was told that Earl

had helped to clear the roads through the mountains and was the first to plan improved thoroughfares in and about Sacramento, as well as at Hangtown. They got him to explain how he originated the Riverside drive down the Sacramento river, that for years was one of the famous roadways of the State. He said that Leland Stanford, C. P. Huntington, Mark Hopkins, and the Crocker Brothers were the first and most liberal subscribers to the fund for the road. It was expected to turn out a losing venture, but much to the surprise of everybody it proved a paying investment. "Good roads always help every important industry and institution of the community, and that is true now as at the beginning," said Earl.

There was a lot of gossip about the "big fire" of July 6, 1856, when Steve Gage saved a printing press by picking it up and carrying it out and throwing it into Hangtown Creek, from which resting place four men were required to rescue it. "I couldn't do that now, boys, so don't start another fire on my account," was Gage's confession and petition.

GAMBLERS AND PREACHERS.

"Hello, Aleck!" cried B. G. Parlow, and Murgotten was called on to tell about the preacher who took a notion to strike out for other diggings and made a raise in an ingenious manner. "Pass me a slug and I'll play you a trick the devil never will," said the minister accosting a group of gamblers. Without a moment's hesitation the gold was handed out and the recipient was about to retire, when he was halted. "Here, tell us about that trick which you say you will play us and the devil never will," insisted one of the contributors. "I'll leave you," was the retort, and the jest was so thoroughly appreciated that the get-away stake was doubled.

"But there's a companion story which goes with that," said Murgotten. "Another preacher in coming around the Horn was on a vessel that was infested with gamblers, and he had nerve enough to tell them what he thought of their trade and their practices, so he finally succeeded in taming the leaders and minimizing their activities. This preacher a couple of years after getting to California had occasion to buy some furniture for his home, and went to a store where he gave his order for a modest outfit of low-priced material. The next day three huge wagons loaded with fine carpets, mahogany tables, upholstered chairs and other furniture of expensive pattern appeared, but the minister refused to accept the things, saying that a mistake had been made. "No mistake at all," said the proprietor of the store who had accompanied the drivers. "This stuff is all for you. You showed yourself to be a true man and a brave man when you reproved those gamblers on ship board. I was one of those gamblers. You certainly gave us a hot deal, but it was the truth and did us good. I resolved to get even with you sometime, if I ever had a chance, and this is my chance. Your sermon made me quit gambling for business and I've got rich. Here's your bill of sale, receipted in full, and if you don't like the furniture you can give it to the poor."

SPECIAL EDITION OF NEWSPAPER.

The "El Dorado Republican and Nugget" got out a special edition in honor of the occasion, and copies of the paper, fresh from the press, were delivered to participants in the banquet while they were still at the table. The leading article was as follows:

More than fifty-nine years ago a gaunt youth of 19 stepped down from an emigrant wagon and took his first look around at the country where he had come to make a fortune. In his pocket was a lone 50-cent piece. Today a kindly-faced aged man stepped down from the tonneau of a luxurious automobile and looked around him at the country where he had laid the foundation for his fortune. It was J. M. Studebaker returning to take perhaps his last look at the scenes of his early struggles.

The auto had drawn up in front of the Ohio House where on the wooden porch stood a score of grizzled men. As Studebaker stepped down from his auto he spied a face in the crowd. "Hello, Newt, you around here yet?" he said, by way of salutation.

"Yes, I'm here yet," answered Newton F. Spencer with his Missouri drawl, "but they call me jedge now, Mr. Studebaker, ye see I'm the Justice of the Peace."

"Huh! what did you ever know about law when you and Hank Monk used to stop in the road and decide with your fists which of your stages was going to back up to let the other pass?" exclaimed Studebaker in jocular tone.

"And you, too, Charley Von Weidierwachs, where's that rip-snortin' Jayhawk, Blackhawk, Mohawk father of yours?" asked Studebaker, shaking hands with a bent figure, beneath whose black hat hung locks of silver gray.

"City Clerk Weatherwax, if you please;" he drew himself up with a mock show of pride, "that name bothered me worse than all tarnation, so I had to change it."

"Well, this town hasn't changed," Studebaker paused to glance about him as he shook hands with the men who were young and full of hope when he first came here.

"And where's Mike Mayer; one of the men who worked with me?" he asked.

Studebaker was told. A few minutes later he was driven up to a white painted cottage and was shown inside. His visit must be brief, he knew.

"Is tnat you, Wheelbarrow John?" a tremulous voice asked the question as a thin and emaciated hand came out from beneath the coverlet and groped for a hand to press in greeting.

"Yes, it's I, Mike," answered Studebaker as he looked into the sightless eyes and drawn face of Michael Mayer.

There was feeling in his voice as Studebaker said, "I must go now, Mike."

They clasped hands for a minute more—these two relics of the days of '49—one worth millions and the other—well, not so rich.

"Goodbye, Mike," Studebaker's voice was unsteady as he released the withered hand.

"Good-bye, John," the other's voice quavered.

Before Studebaker would sit down to the banquet in honor of his return to Hangtown he must see some of the old places he knew. He saw not many. Hangtown was swept by fire while he was here in the early days; it was destroyed again many years after he left. But the old-timers who rode alongside of him pointed out the place where he went to work for Joe Hinds to make wheelbarrows for $10 apiece.

CHARACTERISTIC OF JOE HINDS.

Studebaker said: "Yes, boys, I was here in the fire of 1856. You will remember that we had to abandon the old hand fire-engine in the street, and we took to the hillside, I running for dear life to reach our little shop with our home and all our belongings in the back end, above Stony Point. When I got there the fire was also there. I got hold of my old trunk, which contained all my wardrobe, trinkets, relics and some gold specimens. I started up the hill, with my treasure, but had to abandon it on account of the great heat. After the fire the only things left were the gold specimens and the clothes on my back. But nobody seemed to be discouraged, and none shedding tears. We were right cheerful with our campfires on the hillside, cooking our grub over the coals, and then taking our night's slumber in our blankets under a manzanita bush or a pine tree. A new town went up like magic. I must here give you one of Mr. Hinds' characteristics. We had got our new shop up, and the roof on, but the sides were all open. It was our first night's sleep in our bunks in our new home. Very early in the morning I was awakened by loud cries of "Murder! Murder!" You will remember how in early days the Chinamen were to be seen carrying heavy loads with a pole and a basket at each end. One of these Chinamen was doing the shouting, and Hinds, who was first awakened by the cry for help, ran out in his night shirt to see what the trouble was. There was a big rowdy with a queue of a Chinaman over his shoulder, and pulling the poor Chinaman around, his rice and other belongings scattered all over the street. Hinds, in his night clothes, jumped on the big duffer and he and the Chinaman had him down and were beating the life out of him. If I had not gone to his rescue they might have killed him, they were so indignant. That spontaneous act of protection by Hinds on behalf of a friendless and defenseless human being brought to our shop hundreds of dollars, as Chinamen from all over the district not only brought their picks to us to be sharpened, but they also bought new ones from us."

Those old days came back as he looked reverently at that spot, almost sacred in his eyes.

There were not enough of the old timers to be found to make a showing at the banquet table but their sons and kin were at the gathering.

A SIXTY-YEAR OLD JOURNAL

The "Mountain Democrat," a newspaper published in Placerville more than sixty years, and to which Studebaker subscribed the first day of his arrival, contained the following account of the reception:

Tuesday, April 16, as per previous announcement, J. M. Studebaker, the millionaire manufacturer of South Bend, Indiana, arrived in Placerville, accompanied by a party of El Dorado County pioneers, to once again look upon the

little town, where as a young man he laid the foundation
for his fortune. The party, occupying two automobiles,
were met a short distance down the road by the Mayor and
a committee of citizens and members of the Board of Trade
and escorted into town, where several hours were spent in
driving to points familiar to the distinguished visitor, and
a stop was made at the Mayer home where he called upon
his old associate, Mike Mayer, whose health is so feeble that
he was unable to be present at the banquet.

Mine host, F. P. Merrill, chose as the most appropriate
color for decoration, the golden yellow of the field poppy,
combined with woodwardia ferns; and these were used
in profusion in the hotel entrance, lobby, and dining-room,
where a most tasteful arrangement of the same brilliant
flower adorned each banquet table. The menus were unique
and representative of early day history; the famous "Hangtown Tree," and the first wheelbarrow composing the cover
design.

F. F. Barss acted as toastmaster and introduced Mr.
Studebaker, who entertained the guests present with reminiscences, beginning with his trip across the plains, his
arrival in Hangtown, the construction of his first wheelbarrow, and his experiences up to the present time. Stephen
T. Gage of Oakland, who is well-known here, spoke of his
early experiences in the old town, to which, until recently,
he had made annual return visits. He was followed by
A. P. Murgotten of San Jose, who for many years was
editor of "The Pioneer." His parents are lying in the
cemetery here, and his memories of Placerville are the
tenderest. During the course of his remarks he called the
names of the pioneers who have crossed the Great Divide.

A poem on Hangtown Tree of 1853, which appeared in
the Placerville papers at that time was read. Next came
a song, "The Days of '49," by D. W. Earl, which was loudly
applauded.

WENT TO THE OLD WHEELWRIGHT SHOP.

Studebaker retraced the steps which in days of yore
led to the scene of his daily toil. He visited the old
shop where with such rude implements as the place afforded he had worked at his trade. He shook hands with
the bronzed and bearded men bending over the anvils
and the benches, saying that he took delight in watching
the work go on as it did under his personal guidance so
many years ago and marveled that there was so little
change. The same old wagons, it almost seemed, were
standing in front to be mended, the same old tools, some

of which possibly he had beaten into shape at this primitive forge, were in the racks above the battered old anvil.

Studebaker was glad to note the air of prosperity about the town. He knew that it had experienced seasons of depression, like most places in the country, and he said it was pleasing to see Placerville again on the up grade, not only in respect to the mining situation, but also in the matter of better conditions for all sorts of business. The development of the fruit-growing industry in the uplands he regarded as giving assurance of stability to all the foothill regions, and particularly to the country tributary to Placerville.

"Boys, I never did better work in my life than I did in this shop," was his parting remark. A rusty hammer, which he recognized as one used by him for years, and which he had fashioned for a particular purpose out of a bar of steel, was handed to him, and he bore it away for a memento. Specimens of gold quartz, and placer dust and nuggets were presented to Studebaker as souvenirs, but they were not as highly prized as was this ancient hammer.

UNIQUE MENU CARD.

The dining room of the Ohio House where the banquet was served had been elaborately decorated. The tables held bouquets of wild flowers, and the walls of the room were banked with yellow poppies against a solid background of ferns. The invocation was said by the Rev. E. E. Clark. The menu card, on which was emblazoned a picture of a man swinging from a tree, and another representing a man with overalls in boots trundling a wheelbarrow load of gold, was printed after the manner of pioneer typography, the clever imitation winning compliments for the craftsmen of the Placerville "Republican and Nugget" office. The catalogue of eatables was replete with early-day references.

CHUCK LIST.

Chili Gulch Rib Warmer
Sluice Box Tailings, flavored with
Chicken
Highgrade Olives
Spanish Flat Onions
Cedar Ravine Radishes
Coon Hollow Pickles
Sacramento River Salmon paved with
cheese
Indian Diggings Spuds
Tertiary Moisture
Slab of Cow from the States
Bandana Fries with Bug-juice
Lady Canyon Chicken, Hangtown
dressed
Webbertown Murphys
Shirt-tail Bend Peas
Dead Man's Ravine Asparagus
Cemented Gravel a la Emigrant Jane
Butcher Brown Fizz Water
Assorted Nuggets
Amalgam Cheese, Riffle Crackers
Mahala's Delight en tasse
Texas Hill Fruit
Pay Day Smokes   Hard Pan Smokes

Those seated at the banquet table were J. M. Stude-
baker, Charles H. Townsend, Stephen T. Gage, Alexander
P. Murgotten, William Bell, D. W. Earl, Chester N.
Weaver, Thomas B. Richards, J. M. S. Johnson, F. F.

Barss, Charles H. Weatherwax, Ed Christian, R. K. Berry, J. R. Partridge, Tom Stevens, G. H. Thompson, N. F. Spencer, Rev. E. E. Clark, A. J. Blakeley, James Patton, Max Mierson, Dave Simon, Dr. J. Q. Wrenn, Abe Darlington, A. Darlington, A. Baring-Gould, S. S. Inch Sr., M. P. Bennett, George W. Kimball, N. L. Kohn, E. W. Witmer, Frank Goyan, Frank Goyan Jr., B. G. Parlow, Q. Hardy, James Hughes, A. Koletzke, Charles E. Merrell, J. C. O'Donnell, J. F. Limpinsel, N. Fox, Warren Crocker, S. G. Beach, H. K. Marks, Peter Watt, Dr. S. H. Rantz, C. P. Winchell, Adam Brooks, Sam Maginnis, Robert Blair, John Pearson, J. M. Anderson, J. R. Baird, W. S. Kirk, William Parker, George Hilbert, W. H. Ward, Robert B. Baird, Wells Drury.

The Rev. Mr. Clark was called on to read a lettergram received by Mr. Studebaker on his arrival at Placerville. It was from Frederick S. Fish, Studebaker's son-in-law, and president of the Studebaker Corporation, and conveyed the congratulations of the writer and the congratulations of Mr. Studebaker's daughter and granddaughter upon the happy event he was at that moment so successfully celebrating.

POSTAL TELEGRAPH-CABLE COMPANY
NIGHT LETTERGRAM

"New Orleans, La., April 15th, 1912.—J. M. Studebaker, Placerville, Cal: Your daughter, granddaughter and I join in this message. Our regrets that we were prevented from being with you and your friends can't be expressed in words. Our joy that your great desire is accomplished is equally unexpressable. We know how much pleasure you have anticipated and how much strength you have husbanded in respect to the event you and your friends are now celebrating in Old Hangtown. By pluck, perseverance and patience you laid the foundation for your success in business, not alone by accumulation of gold, but industrial and commercial experience which gave you the possibilities for your future which is now largely and magnificently a satisfactorily accomplished fact. If your former old friends and workers now enjoying your hospitality could only know the unfathomable depths of your loving and generous heart, the genial simplicity of your nature, your great desire for the happiness of others they would in double measure appreciate more than the event itself demonstrates how your heart goes out to them and what a grand old man you are. We send our love to you and them and may the benign blessing of a loving God rest on you all and guide each for many years in paths of happiness and contentment.

"FREDERICK S. FISH."

HEARTFELT GREETING.

After the viands had been discussed amid a jovial flow of merry talk, in which recollections of exciting incidents predominated, F. F. Barss, the Toastmaster, said: "It rejoices my soul to participate in this reception to this old friend of mine. He is your friend and mine, and he shows it by returning to the scene of his earliest struggles for the purpose of paying homage to the old place. This pilgrimage is inspired by the high ideals that have ever governed the conduct of our honored host and friend. He is our guest because we have come here for the purpose of welcoming him to our home and hearts. He is our host because we are enjoying his hospitality at this splendid feast. It is a pleasure for us all to again take him by the hand and look into his face, which still wears the same genial smile with which it was lighted when we were young together. I take pleasure in presenting J. M. Studebaker."

THREE CHEERS AND A TIGER.

"Three cheers for Studebaker," called a man at the lower end of the table, and the cheers were given with a will, followed by the "tiger," for which the pioneers of California were famous.

It was some time before the enthusiasm settled sufficiently for the voice of Studebaker to be heard, but finally quiet was restored, and he said:

"Citizens of Placerville and old friends of dear old Hangtown: We have come back to commemorate the

times and the days of old Hangtown. Words fail me
when I attempt to express my love of the early days
when you, my friends, and I were young.

ONLY ONE TO COME BACK.

"No doubt some of you wonder why I am the only one
to ever come back to renew in this way these recollections and to show my regard for you and for the days
of old. Possibly some of them are too busy, and you
know we all do not think alike.

"By coming back and giving you this farewell dinner
it is my desire to show my respect for you, my friends,
and to offer a last tribute to those who have gone before.
We who are here have seen the years that usually span
the term of human existence. We have lived our lives.
We have had its joys and sorrows; its trials and its
triumphs. God created this beautiful world for his children to live in and make more beautiful and better. The
man who goes through his alloted time in this old world
without trying to make it better amounts to little. When
I look upon your kindly faces, that time has touched so
gently, it seems to me, softening and mellowing the
manly lineaments, thoughts come to me of the early
struggles of us all. We shared our burdens together
then more than is the custom now, and all of us were
the better for it; but after all no one knows a man's
life except himself. No one can look into the heart of
his nearest companion and read the secrets. No one can
judge. Therefore we must all be compassionate; we
must be considerate to our associates, making due al-
lowance for mistakes of head or heart—and this we must
all ask of one another.

WILLING TO WORK.

"You will permit me, perhaps, to refer to my own efforts since I left you. It was nearly sixty years ago that
a strong, healthy, robust lad of 19 years arrived here,
and made his first stop almost at the very spot where
we now are. That youngster was myself. He came of
good old Pennsylvania stock, inheriting from his father

and mother a sound body and a willingness to do his
work—whatever it might be—to the best of his ability.
He came with a determination to work out his own des-
tiny.

"It is not necessary to recount the incidents of my
start across the plains, as so many of you took the same
trip. You know how weary and tiresome was the journey.

"The first wagon I ever made was used in the company with which I came across the plains. I did the
woodwork and my brother ironed it, and I gave it to the
company for permission to accompany them to California.
We were more than five months on the road, and landed
in California right up here on this square in August, 1853,
and I had but fifty cents in my pocket. Although that
was my only earthly possession my spirit was not
daunted, for we were all led to believe, as many of you
also believed, that all we had to do was to go out on
the morrow and dig all the gold that the heart could desire. How many of us found out that this was not true!

"Of course a big crowd gathered around us, and while
we were trying to get them to talk about the gold mines
they insisted on asking questions about what had happened in the States since they had heard from their
friends. While the hubbub was going on a man came up
and asked if there was a wagon-maker in the crowd of
new arrivals. They pointed me out and he asked: 'Are
you a wagon-maker?'

BIG AS LIFE WITH FIFTY CENTS.

"'Yes sir,' I answered, as big as life, with my fifty-
cent piece in my pocket. [Laughter.]

"The man was Joe Hinds, whom you all knew and
respected. He offered me a job in his shop, but I replied
that I came to California to mine for gold, and that I
had never thought of taking any other kind of a job.
Hinds turned on his heel and walked off. You all know
that he was a man of few words.

"After he was gone a man whom I afterwards found
out was Dr. Worthem, stepped up and very politely said:
'Will you let me give you a little advice, young man?'

I said yes, and he continued: 'Take that job and take it quick.' [Laughter.]

"His manner impressed me. He said that there would be plenty of time to dig gold, which was not always a sure thing, and that the job just offered me was a mighty fine chance for a stranger.

"I thought it was a pretty good idea, and as there were four of us youngsters who had come together, and all of us were broke, I decided to go to work for the wagon-maker if he would take me.

MADE WHEELBARROWS FOR $10 APIECE.

"I followed Hinds to his shop. It was not above Stony Point, I remember, and was a log house, with the back wall made by digging into the hill. There were coffee-sack bunks in which we slept, and in the middle of the room was a sheet-iron stove on which the cooking was done.

"I explained that I had decided to see what he wanted me to do, and he said he wanted me to make wheelbarrows for the miners. He wanted twenty-five and would pay me $10 apiece. So I began the next morning. The tools were the worst you ever saw, and the only material was pitch-pine lumber. I got along very slow at first, and at noon found that I was hungry. So I went down to the square where there was a big sign, 'Philadelphia Hotel.' You remember that the rule then was to pay a dollar before you went in. But I had no dollar. And my three companions were in the same fix. In talking with Simons, the proprietor, I told him I was from South Bend, Indiana, and found that he was from a place near by. He was Dutch, and I talked some of my Pennsylvania Dutch to him. Finally after I told him that I was working for Hinds he let us go in, and we ate enough for three days. [Laughter.]

"Simons went over to find out from Hinds if we were lying, and he had plenty of time, we staid so long at the table. The other boys were wild to get started at mining, so I took them over to Hinds and got him to trust them for pick and shovel and pan. Simons fixed up

enough grub to last for two days, and the boys started
out to try their luck. The miners had a habit of telling
a tenderfoot to dig almost anywhere except in good
places, just for a joke, and that was the way they treated
my friends. It might have been funny for them, but it
was hard on the boys.

"At the end of the second day I got one wheelbarrow
done. Hinds looked at it. 'What do you call that?' he
asked, puffing his old pipe.

" 'I call it a wheelbarrow,' I answered.

" 'A hell of a wheelbarrow,' was his comment. And
he was correct, for as a matter of fact the wheel was a
little crooked. But I put up the best excuse I could.

" 'You asked me if I was a wagon-maker and I said
I was. I didn't say that I was a wheelbarrow maker; but
I think I can do better on the next one.' He smiled grimly
and said 'Go ahead.' I got myself provided with better
tools and turned out a fair product, making a wheelbarrow
a day. My comrades worked in the mines for a whole
month. and I paid their expenses, but they didn't strike
anything worth while. Then they left, and I never heard
of them from that day to this.

SOME HAD BAD LUCK.

"Just about then we all heard many conversations
something like this: 'Joe, how long you been mining
here?'

" 'Six months.'

" 'How much have you got?'

" 'Not a d—— cent.'

"And so it went. Hundreds and thousands who tried
the mines never made a success. But we who stuck to
steady jobs at good wages and saved our money were sure
of doing well. Joe Hinds and I worked many a night all
night—he making new picks and I repairing stages that
came in late and that had to get out at 6 o'clock in the
morning. It was not always the fault of the mines, how-
ever, that the young fellows failed to make a stake, for
they gambled away their gold dust like so many reckless
sports that they were.

"But I had learned something by experience which kept me from that form of wastefulness. I guess I'll have to make a confession even if the joke is on me. At home I didn't know one card from another. My good mother, the mother of thirteen children, who spun the yarn, and wove the cloth and made the clothing for the family, with the help of the children, had taught us to be honest and to avoid temptation.

HONEST CONFESSION GOOD FOR THE SOUL.

"This dear good mother just before I started, sewed $65 in gold in a belt which I buckled round my body. When we got to Council Bluffs on the Missouri river we had to stop for three days, and were soon beset by three-card monte sharpers and their cappers. The cappers gave us glowing descriptions of how they were winning money every day from these helpless gamblers, and they asked, 'What is the use of going to California when you can win all the gold you want right here?' showing handfuls of money. They took in the smartest boy in our crowd, a printer, and let him win a few times, and he saw how the cappers were getting rich at the expense of the bankers. It was really too bad, of course, but he explained that we might as well have our share, as the poor fellows were bound to go broke any how. The young printer posted all who had money about the splendid chance, and swore us to secrecy, not to tell the bosses. So he led the attack, saying that we would go in and bust the bank. 'When I bet $5 you bet $10,' he explained, because he didn't want the dealers to know that he was getting all the money, or that we were in any way associated. He even explained that he didn't dare to win every time, though his system was so perfect that he could if he wanted to. Well, I went in with the rest, and for awhile looked on. But the other fellows, mostly cappers, as I afterwards learned, were gathering in the money so fast that I got scared for fear it would all be gone, and I thought there wouldn't be anything left for me.

"So I went out and got behind the building and took off my belt, and cut it open, taking out the $65 my good mother had sewed in there. As quickly as possible I began to bet, but somehow the system didn't work, or luck was against me. To make a long story short, or rather a short story shorter, we all left our money with those sharpers. And that's how I happened to have only 50 cents when I went to making wheelbarrows for Hinds.

AN EMIGRANT KILLED.

"We went back to the camp and told the bosses, and they were mad because we didn't let them know in advance about the gambling, so that they might have warned us against the certainty of being robbed. Then they asked if there was any fight in us, and we all said yes. So the arrangement was made to go and clean out the gamblers and get our money back, as we were convinced we had a right to do. But when we reached the town, which was about two miles from our camp, the place was all commotion and uproar.

"An emigrant had been killed the night before and all gambling was stopped and the three-card monte dealers had disappeared.

CARD-SHARP HANGED FOR MURDER.

"The emigrants, numbering from 500 to 1000, rounded up all the gamblers, catching them as they tried to escape, and a friend of the dead man who had seen him last in company with a gambler was asked if he could identify the gambler. All the three card-sharpers and their cappers were stood up in a row, and the dead emigrant's friend pointed out one, saying 'That's the man.' We boys recognized him as the dealer who had robbed us at three-card monte. A jury of twelve men was sworn in and after hearing the testimony the prisoner was found guilty and was hanged right there. With the rope round his neck he made a complete confession, saying that he committed the murder because the dead man made him believe that he had a large sum of money in his tent, but that all he round was half a dollar. The convicted mur-

derer warned us all against gambling, 'My dying advice
to all you boys is to never play cards for money; never
gamble or bet on the other man's game.'

LESSON THAT DID GOOD.

"That was the best lesson I ever had. Whenever
some proposition like that would come up, with a gamble
in it, whetner in business or otherwise, I would always
say to myself: 'What a fool. Why should I take the
risk? Why should I bet:' for that's what it amounts to
when you go into a thing that you don't understand.

"You all who have lived here have seen hundreds of
young men bring pints of gold dust and nuggets to town
Saturday nights, and many a Monday morning I have
had to lend them enough to get grub for the week.

"So I say that was the lesson of my life. One was
enough for me. Never bet on another man's game.
Whenever you do you are sure to get the worst of it.

WHEELBARROW LOADED WITH COIN.

"There's another story in which you will all be in-
terested, and it seems right to tell it here, because it
is called up by looking at that picture of a wheelbarrow
which graces our menu card. When the Adams Express
Company failed I had $3000 in the bank—all the money
I had in the world. Hinds, my partner, had $22,000 in
the same bank. I remember that it was 2 o'clock in the
afternoon that the bank was closed, and we all knew
that if it didn't open the next morning the boys would
come in and tear up everything, provided they thought
there was any money in the place. That's where Hinds
and his level head came in. He knew that the express
people would try to get their money out that night, for
the failure was caused by lack of money elsewhere, and
not at Hangtown. You all remember that the bank
backed right up against Hangtown Creek, and without
saying a word to anybody Hinds made up his plan. He
hid in the brush back of the bank just across the creek,
and watched.

"Sure enough, just as he expected, he saw the express people creep out of the building at about 2 o'clock

in the morning with the bags of gold. He trailed them
and saw them put the money in old Joe Douglas' safe.
The rest was easy for Hinds. He waked me up and told
me what had been done, and said he was going to levy
an attachment on tne safe, and from what he saw he was
confident there was enough to pay us both, so he asked
me if I wanted to stand in on the attachment suit. Of
course I did, and we got out the papers bright and early.
You can depend on it we didn't waste any time. Douglas,
the old sinner, denied that the money was in his safe,
but the officer found it and served the attachment, and
as there was no defense we got the coin in short order,
every dollar of it, while hundreds of others, after long
waiting, received only 15 to 30 per cent. Hinds threw
that money into a wheelbarrow and trundled it through
the streets of Hangtown. So the picture on the bill of
fare is most appropriate. It tells a story. [Applause.]

TRAINED BY WESTERN EXPERIENCE.

"You see there are so many things that combine to
make success in life. As I have explained, I probably
never would have made my start if it had not been for
my various experiences in old Hangtown and on the frontier, where lessons are burned into the hearts and minds
of men, in a way that they cannot forget. I have had but
two rules. The first was to work hard, and the second
was never to buy anything that I couldn't afford. My
good wife and I put our first baby to sleep in a rude
rocking chair. For the next we got a $3.50 cradle, and
then when a boy came along in ten years I paid $50 for
a baby cab. And it wasn't extravagance, because I could
afford it. [Applause.]

"You probably know that the company with which I
am connected has enjoyed a certain measure of success.
We have a large factory and employ 10,000 men. It was
the money that I got out of that busted bank and the
savings of five years that went into the business of Studebaker Brothers, and so far as I am concerned it all came
from the start that I got in old Hangtown. Why shouldn't

I have a love for the old place? Wouldn't I deserve to be called an ingrate if I didn't? [Applause.]

YOU GET OUT OF LIFE WHAT YOU PUT IN IT.

"God made these bodies of ours, and gave us intelligence to choose right from wrong, and it is up to us to appreciate the lives that we are permitted to live. After all, life is what you get out of it, and you get out of it what you put in; whether of service or love or the consciousness of trying to do your duty. Money doesn't make happiness. Honesty of purpose is the mainstay. Upright character, sincere affections, trying to help those who have not been so fortunate—these go to the making of a contented mind, a cheerful disposition, a happy life. Pardon me if I do not speak these words as fluently as some others would do. They spring from my heart and I give them utterance as they come.

"This is my farewell dinner to old comrades and friends, to commemorate the events of our lives in old Hangtown. We shall never meet again 'this side of God and dawn.' But there is nothing to hinder us from realizing God's promise. We may meet again in the happy future.

"Good bye, dear friends, good bye and may God bless you with the best of life here and a world of peace hereafter."

Three cheers were given for John Studebaker, the guests arising and joining with a will in the tribute of respect for the honored visitor.

STEVE GAGE RECEIVES OVATION.

Stephen T. Gage was called on by the Toastmaster and was greeted enthusiastically when he arose.

He was introduced as one who had always been honored in Placerville, having been elected to the California Legislature from that district in 1857, and served as City Marshal in '58 and '59, afterwards engaging in the freighting business between Placerville and Virginia City, and for years held a prominent part in the development of Nevada; finally returning to California.

TO OLD HANGTOWN OR BUST

"Thoughts crowd on my memory so that my words cannot express them. There is such a flood of recollections that I despair of telling you what I feel in this presence. Here among these venerable men I seem to see the events of years pass in review, but the pictures must be painted by others. The best I can hope to do is to sketch some of the scenes which came under my observation.

"Thousands upon thousands came here in search of gold. Their like was never seen before. Through the main thoroughfare of Placerville, past the doors of the building in which we now are, swept this vast concourse of people. Lured by gold they braved the dangers of the plains, the hardships of the frontier, the toil of the mines.

"You will not object if on a day like this I refer to my personal experience. Sixty years ago at this very moment I was on the plains. That is easy to say, but unless you have passed through similar experience it is hard to understand. Little do they know of the trials, the tribulations of the emigrants who crossed the plains. Few realize the perils which those people faced without flinching. It was from such hazardous experiences that sprang the intrepid determination which marked that generation. It was a condition of mind; a resolve to win or die trying. [Applause.]

SCENES NEVER DESCRIBED.

"The experience of those who crossed the plains has never been written and never will be. No person ever did or can describe those scenes. It was estimated in round numbers 100,000 crossed the Missouri river in 1852, and for the most of those Hangtown was the objective point; the only place they had heard of. "To Old Hangtown or Bust," was their slogan. How many fell by the way never will be known. Of those who got through about 15 per cent branched off and went to Oregon. The remainder came to California, and almost everyone of them passed through old Hangtown. My friend Studebaker says it took him more than five months to make the trip. I beat him, because it took me just 100

days from St. Jo, Missouri to Hangtown. The reason
I beat him so much was because he drove horses and I
came with a team of oxen, and engineered it myself.
Cattle always out-traveled horses on that long and trying
journey. Let me tell you how I am so certain about the
time. I kept a diary, and I have it yet to prove what I
say, and don't have to refer to Bill Jones, who is dead,
or Sam Smith, or anybody else to back me up.

WHEELS WITH STUDEBAKER GUARANTY.

"I had the honor of buying and using one of those
first wheelbarrows made by our friend Studebaker. You
will notice that I say honor, and not pleasure, for to tell
the truth it was not a pleasure to run a wheelbarrow in
the gold diggings. I will add that it was a good wheelbarrow, honestly made, strong and well put together in
every part, and it was worth what it cost, every cent.
It had the personal guaranty of Studebaker behind it,
which stood for sterling quality then as it does now, in
every product which comes from that marvelous hive of
industry at South Bend. [Applause.]

"That habit of turning out prime articles which Studebaker had impressed on him then has stuck to him and
those connected with him, and is their most valuable asset.
[Applause.]

WHERE GOLD WAS DISCOVERED.

"El Dorado county was the empire county of the state
in those days. It was at Sutter's mill, at Coloma, on the
American river, only eight miles from here that gold was
discovered by John Marshall.

"When I struck this camp I was barely 21 years of
age, and I looked on anybody who was ten years my
senior as a venerable person, to be respected for his experience and wisdom. Therefore I sought the company
of such men as William Cooper and George W. Swan,
and tried to gain something from their superior position.
The pleasantest decade of my life was passed right here,
and then I went to Nevada to help organize it first as a

territory, and then as a state, but always I have been glad to come back, and I am happy to be with you today.

FLAMES SWEPT MINING TOWNS.

"In the metropolis there is an idea that all the energy, character and worth of the country are monopolized by that community. That is a mistake. San Francisco got not only its money, its real financial sinews, but its best people from this and other similar places. Talk about destructive fires developing character! Can you tell me of any mining town on the coast that was not swept out of existence time and again, and there was never a squeal. None of us ever thought of calling on anybody else for help. We stood together, and the people showed true grit every time. They just picked their flint and resolved to try again. [Applause and voices, 'That's so, you bet.']

"Often I have intended to write a book of pleasant recollections, but I never seem to find the time. It would be a joy to review those heroic days when the genuine feeling of fraternity ruled the land. Then every man's word was his bond. You could leave the gold in the pan and go to dinner and know to a certainty that you would find it all there when you came back. Then we had no insane asylums, but took care of the few unfortunates in our own helpful way. There were no state prisons, and none were needed. Now we have two and ought to have as many more. [Laughter.]

"Then, as now, California's chief claim for precedence rested on our climate, our scenery and our health-producing conditions. The presence of so many of the old timers at this gathering today emphasizes the life-prolonging qualities of our unequaled climate." [Applause, followed by three cheers for Steve Gage.]

SHEAF OF THRICE-TOLD TALES.

Alexander P. Murgotten favored the assembly with a bouquet of humorous stories, describing some of the odd happenings of the pioneer days. There was a storm of applause when he mentioned that he was commissioned to convey to the devoted group the best wishes of William

A. January, their respected friend and neighbor, now in his 87th year. He deeply regretted that he was unable to be present.

MARK TWAIN CHALLENGED TO A DUEL.

"It was while at Hangtown that Professor W. Frank Stewart, noted mining expert and scientist, inven'.d a new earthquake register or seismograph, but Mark Twain wrote up for the Virginia City Enterprise a fake account of its first triai, pretending that a mangy hog scratching his back against the clapboards of Professor Stewart's cabin threw that learned gentleman into a paroxysm of fear, and caused him to report the occurrence of a terrible earthquake which never happened. Mark meant it for a jest, but Stewart took it as a deadly insult, and challenged the joker to a duel, refusing to be placated with anything less than a retraction and an apology.

"Among the venerated names of old Hangtown stands that of Penn Johnson, that .brilliant genius, who introduced to this community the ancient and honorable order famous throughout the world as E Clampsus Vitus. [Laughter and applause.] Only pioneers will understand this reference to the most elaborate and stupendous josh organization that ever was known on earth.

"I wish to thank our venerable host for this opportunity which we have of meeting together today. I knew our friend fifty-nine years ago when, I believe, 50 cents was the extent of his worldly wealth, while today he is one of the Captains of Industry, head of one of the largest manufacturing industries of this country, if not of the world. I have watched his rise and taken pleasure in his achievement and I know I express the sentiments of all here present when I hope he may be spared many years to enjoy the fruits of his industry.

OLD BULL RING ON THE HILL.

"When I received my invitation to be here, many reminiscences began to pass before my vision. I could see the old bull ring on the hill where the school house now stands It was erected by Ben. Nickerson. I remember the last exhibition, neither the bear nor bull would fight. The crowd got mad, tore down the pen, killed the bear and rolled it down the steep hill. The mob led the bull through the streets, beating him. As he passed my father's store on main street, the bull got tired of the fun and turned and kicked one of the tormentors in the forehead, laying him out. He was taken into our store and old Dr. Worthem brought him to.

"Do any of you boys remember the jack-screw our dentists used to pull teeth with? I do, and after being pulled around the room, the tooth broke and for forty years I could never be induced to go near a dentist.

"You all remember the prominent merchant, who represented your county once in the Legislature, who said, as a troop of soldiers were passing through town, that 'General Canby has gone on ahead in an avalanche.'

WAR-TIME THERMOMETER.

"You certainly all remember old Dr. Childs, who during our late unpleasantness was our war thermometer. On the arrival of the stage, if the news was good for the Union side, he walked up the street with his old plug-hat on the back of his head; but if the Rebs had won a fight he went along with his hat over his eyes.

SCORNED THE TOLL-BRIDGE.

"When my father and Charles P. Jackson, of Mud Springs, first came to Hangtown in 1850, they walked from Sacramento. At Webber creek they crossed over on old Morrill's toll-bridge. When they got over 50 cents was demanded. Mr. Jackson said he'd be d——d if he'd pay it, and went back and crossed over on the rocks, there not being water enough in the creek to float a trout.

"I sold papers for Alex. Hunter in 1852-3-4 and ate Jim Hume's and Charley Hilbert's pies and cakes.

"An amusing trick was played on our old County Judge, James Johnson. In the Mountain Democrat office was a brass mould used for making rollers for the press, about three feet long. The boys fixed it up as a telescope to see the comet. In one end they put a French picture, and then waited for the old judge. You can imagine the wrath of the staid old judge, and to say comet to him for a year was good for thirty days in the cooler.

"The tenderfoot has always doubted the story that gold dust could be left out in those days unmolested; but I have seen many buckets and pans of gold from the clean-ups and nobody in sight. The lesson of the Hangtown tree made everybody honest.

WOMEN MINERS PROTECTED THEIR CLAIM.

"With the mention of a miners' meeting held by women I shall close my rambling remarks. It seems that the few women that were here in the early '50's, my mother among them, had a mining claim near the mouth of Log Cabin Ravine. One day some Chinamen jumped the claim. The women called a miners' meeting and decided to eject Mr. Chinaman. They went over in a body, threw the Chinks and their tools out and told them to 'git,' and they 'got' while a number of white men stood by and enjoyed the sport.

"But before I tire you out I want to call the roll of many of the familiar names of those I knew in the days of old, the days of gold, all of whom have passed 'over the divide' ahead of us.

TRIBUTE TO ABSENT BROTHERS.

"One of the most beautiful parts of the Order of Elks' ritual is that devoted to their 'Absent Brothers,' as they drink the Eleven O'Clock toast. So now let us pause in our festivities for a moment with bated breath while we call the roll of our departed comrades, many of whom sleep profoundly beneath the trees on yon hillside, while the swaying pines sing solemn requiems over their graves, while others are awaiting the trumpet's sound in hallowed ground in nearly every state and country under the sun."

The roll call of the dead was then read as follows: John Hume, James B. Hume, E. B. Carson, Walter Burrell, Alex. Hunter, Dave Johns, John O'Donnell Cornelius Russell, Matt Metzler, Cyrus Bartlett, Judge Jas. Johnson,

Wm. M. Donohue Dr. E. A. Kunkler, Geo. Burnham, John
Kirk, Col. Wm. Jones, Geo. W. Stout, Theo. Wichman, Ben.
F. Post, John Mell, Geo. H. Gilbert, Dr. Ira Glynn, Jos. M.
Staples, A. A. Van Voorhees, Henry Van Voorhees, H. C.
Sloss, John Roy, Wm. Lacy, Brewst Herrick, C. W. Mount-
joy, Walter M. Reynolds, J. L. Perkins, Fred Hunger, Judge
Irvine, Judge Bush, Judge S. W. Sanderson, Henry Ra-
phael, A. Tannewald, D. K. Newell, D. W. Gelwicks, Thos.
Downing, Dr. Robert Rankin, B. P.Rankin, Dr. S. F. Childs,
Dr. Worthem, Theo. F. Tracey, Dr. W. H. Stone, W. Frank
Stewart, R. T. McBride, Thos. Castyle, L. W. Rumsey,
Thos. H. Williams, Hank Monk, D. DeGolia, John Car-
theche, Thos. A. Springer, A. W. Bee, Fred. A. Bee, Dr. P.
Chamberlain, Col. C. C. Batterman, J. B. Crandall, R. P.
Culver, Chas. E. McLain, A. H. Reid, Jack McDougal, Jo.
W. Hinds, Oscar Greeley, Rev. McGonigle, Judge Brum-
field, John White, Dr. Ober, Herman Doyle, Bush Dixson,
E. G. Parker, S. A. Grantham, Judge Ogden Squires, David
Newbauer, Edgar Bogardus, Rev. Wm. Freer, Rev. Isaac
Diehl, Abe Seligman, Samuel Ensminger, M. Laverty, Robt.
Chalmers, Judge I. B. Vernon, Nelson Flake, Seth Loveless,
J. Q. A. Ballard, W. M. Hale, Joel Kay, Jas. McCall, Solon
McFarland, Samuel Wallace, Chas. W. Trueman, Geo.
Waite, B. F. Wright, Jos. McMurray, W. H. Bruner, J. M.
Cruz, J. M. Weymouth, A. Mierson, M. Simons, W. H. Tay-
lar, D. S. Smith, G. W. Hunter, C. C. Chapman, Geo. W.
Parsons, J. R. Munson, H. C. Murgotten, John Huntress, A.
C. Arvidson, John M. Howell, A. H. Saxton, A. L. Gordnow,
R. H. Black, A. Bell, S. B. Alderson, S. B. Wallace, Miller
Brothers, Martin Alhoff, John Merchant, Charles Shafer,
Major Ormsby, Jerry Chapman, Jerry Johnson, Col. W. W.
Gift, D. W. C. Spencer, W. K. Creque, George Trimble, H.
T. Plant, Joseph Todd, Col. Jack Lewis, H. B. Pierce, A.
Halfmyer, Samuel Doncaster, Richard Doncaster, Jas. W.
Seeley, Thos. Coppinger, Dr. Hinman, Dr. Burr, R. Cunning-
ham, S. A. Berry, Ned. Welton, B. T. Hunt, George Gordon,
Fred K. Krauth, Alfred Merrill, A. H. Spence, A. C. Henry,
Jas. Blair, John Blair, Walter Webster Sr., O. H. Burnham.
J. W. Shanklin, J. P. Wunderlich, Phil Teare, W. H. Brown

Wm. T. Gibbs, W. S. Buns, Jos. T. Middleton, Powell Crosley, Maj. B. B. Bee, John D. Van Eaton, Thos. Hogsett, W. W. Stewart, John Brewster, Dr. Obed Harvey, Judge Duden, Jesse Yarnell, H. C. Hooker, Dave Holland, D. W. Leon, J. C. McCallum, Dr. Asa Clark, John Conness, Judge Aaron Bell, John Dollison, Dr. W. E. Echelroth, A. St. Clair Denver, Gen. Denver, Charley Crowell, H. F. Page, Chas. P. Jackson, F. A. Hornblower, W. L. Marple, Wm. H Rogers, J. P. Martin. Pat. Lynch, Dr. 'J. E. Kunkler, Eli George, Dr. Thos Hall, Wm. Alverson, John McF. Pearson, Chas. Hilbert, Bronson Brothers, N. Parlow, H. B. House, Geo. C. Raney, Lee McKinstry, Col. Jackie Johnson, George Looney, Dr. I. S. Titus, Peter B. Quinlin, Dr. George Fitch, John J. Cullen, Robert Bell, Mark Levison, Doc Adams, Sammy Lewis, Judge J. C. Pennie, J. F. Pinkham, John Walls. George M. Condee, L. B. Hopkins, D. L. Munson, H. J. McKusick, Capt. W. H. Smith, Dr. Lunborg, Jas. J. Green. Robert White, Jos. White. Rudolph Seligman, Sol. Moore, Jas. E. Bowie, J. M. Grantham, Joseph Fisher, F. H. Harmon, G. J. Carpenter, William Macumsey, Colonel Simon Alter, John Waters, Charles B. Pettit, Dr. C. C. Cook, F. W. Bye, Andrew Kennedy, Michael Sherrer, John Fountain, Dave Buel, Gabe D. Hall, Judge Humphreys. A. Benham, who lost his life in the big fire of 1856; W. M Carey, of the Carey House, C. J. Arvidson, watchmaker, and Thos. Nugent, known in those days as Count Nugent, the first postmaster of Hangtown.

HANGTOWN TREE, 1853.

Mr. Studebaker refreshed the memories of his venerable guests by reading the lines of Joe Fisher, an old South Bender, composed when Bruce Herrick was planning to fell the tree which had made Hangtown renowned.

Herrick, spare that tree!
Let not its branches fall;
Here let it always be
A warning to us all.

For it was in forty nine,
        When our good town yet was young
Three men for murder vile
        Upon that tree were hung.

Yes, on this same old tree
        These miscreants met their doom;
Keep it, for all to see—
        As a grave-tree o'er their tomb.

This tree let always stand!
        For 'tis of great renown;
Then, Herrick, stay thy hand;
        Spare this relic of our town.

But the plaintive wail of Fisher's muse was unavailing,
as the tree was chopped down, and Mr. Studebaker testi-
fied that he helped the axmen, and also carried brick and
mortar used to construct the building which stands in
good repair today, and for nearly sixty years has been
thronged with the eager populace of that lively burgh.

ELOQUENT TRIBUTE TO THE PIONEERS.

"The Song to the Pioneers," by Judge C. C. Good-
win was then rendered with great feeling.

"Sing to the Pioneers tonight!
        Sing to the little band
Who, when with youth each eye was bright
        And strong each good right hand,
Commenced with songs their mighty toil
        To build up new estates,
To lay secure in virgin soil
        The cornerstones of States.

"In every vale, on every hill,
        Are graves of Pioneers;
They mark where rugged hearts grew still,
        And where, as swept the years,

Worn out at length by toil and care
  By hardship too much tried,
They gave the mighty struggle o'er,
  Folded their arms and died.

"There's but a little remnant left—
  Of thousands, but a few;
And every year some hearts are cleft,
  Some disappear from view.
The hands that from above are reached
  To beckon them away,
Exceed the hands that are outstretched
  On earth to make them stay.

"Then sing we to the dear 'Old Boys,'
  Soft may ther life-streams run;
Soothed be their age with sacred joys,
  And when their work is done,
May they with youth renewed awake
  Upon a flower-crowned shore,
Where royal hearts shall never break,
  And peace reign evermore.

L'ENVOI.

"Sing to the Old Boys—sing to them tonight,
They who on the rude frontier made their gallant fight.
They who in the wilds raised thrones to law and right,
Sing to the Old Boys—sing to them tonight."

THE DAYS OF OLD, THE DAYS OF GOLD.

After that was the singing of "The Day of Forty-nine,"
the audience joining in the chorus. This ancient classic
is appropiately a part of every program such as that
at Hangtown.

"Oh, here you see old Tom Moore, a relic of by-gone days,
And a bummer, too, they call me now, but what care I for
    praise.
For my heart is filled with thoughts of yore, and oft do
    I repine
For the days of old, for the days of gold, yes, the days of
    forty-nine.

"I'd comrades then who loved me well, a jovial, saucy crew,
There were some hard nuts I must confess, but still
    they were brave and true,
Who'd never flinch, whate'er the pinch, would never fret
    nor whine,
But like good old bricks, they stood the kicks, in the days
    of forty-nine.

"There was Kentuck Bill, I knew him well, a fellow so
    full of tricks,
At a poker game he was always there, and as heavy, too,
    as bricks;
He'd play you draw, he'd ante a slug, and go a hatful blind,
But in a game with death, poor Bill lost his breath, in the
    days of forty-nine.

"There was Monte Pete, I'll ne'er forget, for the luck he
    always had,
He'd deal for you both night and day, or as long as you
    had a scad.
One night a pistol laid him out, 'twas his last 'lay out,' in
    fine,
It caught Pete sure, right dead in the door, in the days of
    forty-nine.

"There was New York Jake, a butcher-boy, so fond of
    getting tight,
And whenever Jake got on a spree he was spoiling for
    a fight.
One day he ran ag'in a knife in the hands of old Bob Cline,
So over Jake we held a wake, in the days of forty-nine.

"There was Hackensack Jim, who could out-roar a buffalo
    bull, you bet,
He roared all day and he roared all night, and I guess he's
    roaring yet.
One night he fell in a prospect hole—'twas a roaring bad
    design,
For in that hole Jim roared out his soul, in the days of
    forty-nine.

"There was poor lame Jess, a hard old case, who never
   would repent,
Jess never missed a single meal, and he never paid a cent;
But poor old Jess, like all the rest, did to death at last
   resign,
For in his bloom he went up the flume, in the days of
   forty-nine.

"Of all the comrades I had then, not one remains to toast,
They have left me here in my misery, like some poor
   wandering ghost,
And as I stray from place to place, folks call me a trav-
   eling sign,
Saying, 'Here's old Tom Moore, a bummer sure, from the
   days of forty-nine.' "

Max Mierson, President of the Board of Trade, on behalf of the citizens and friends, proposed the toast, "Speed
the Parting Guest," bespeaking the good will and kindly
wishes of the community for the man whom they were
proud to refer to as their former townsman.

After singing "Auld Lang Syne," the final hand clasps
were given and the company separated, many never to
meet again.

The return trip from Placerville was begun as the sun
was sinking. The rhythmic throbbing of the automobiles
fretted the echoes of the hills and canyons. At the foot
of a sharp grade a heavy, slow-winged night-hawk swung
athwart the gathering shadows. An owl spoke from the
dismantled casement of a tumble-down stage station.

   "Above the pines the moon was slowly drifting,
      The river sang below;
   The dim Sierras, far beyond, uplifting
      Their minarets of snow "

www.ingramcontent.com/pod-product-compliance
Lightning Source LLC
LaVergne TN
LVHW021548080426
835509LV00019B/2902